TIM BURTON

Tim
BUR

Ron Magliozzi
Jenny He

THE MUSEUM OF MODERN ART

Contents

Artist's Statement

Growing up in Burbank, there wasn't much of a museum culture. I never visited one until I was a teenager (unless you count the Hollywood Wax Museum). I occupied my time going to see monster movies, watching television, drawing, and playing in the local cemetery. Later, when I did start frequenting museums, I was struck by how similar the vibe was to the cemetery. Not in a morbid way, but both have a quiet, introspective, yet electrifying atmosphere. Excitement, mystery, discovery, life, and death all in one place. So all these years later, to have this exhibition, to be showing things — some of which weren't meant to ever be seen, or are just pieces of the larger picture — is very special to me.

Tim Burton

Foreword

The Museum of Modern Art has been presenting the art and artists of cinema in its galleries since May 1939, when it opened *George Méliès: A Film Pioneer*. Over the seventy years following, the Museum's Titus Theater galleries have been the site of more than eighty exhibitions on the work of film studios such as Pixar, Warner Bros., Universal, and UPA, and of filmmakers D.W. Griffith, Ernie Gehr, Alfred Hitchcock, Ray Harryhausen, John and Faith Hubley, Pier Paolo Pasolini, Roberto Rossellini, and David O. Selznick, among others. With *Tim Burton* the Museum stages its largest, most comprehensive monographic show to date on a filmmaker, one who has distinguished himself internationally as among the foremost auteur voices of his time.

The exhibition of Burton's studies, drawings, photographs, and models provides access to personal, virtually unknown work that until now he has kept to himself. We are fortunate that in addition to being a director, producer, artist, photographer, author, collector, and pop culture enthusiast, Burton is also an archivist of his own career, and we are honored to be the first institution to introduce the majority of these works to the public. Their display offers an intimate experience of his sensibility, more so perhaps than his interviews and even his films. Undiluted, provocative, and humorous, his doodles, sketches, drawings, and paintings are the raw material from which he draws inspiration as a filmmaker. They allow us to appreciate his range of expressive styles and mastery of multiple mediums, they give us insight into his artistic influences, and they provide us with a new perspective on his gothic and surrealist motifs and core themes of childhood alienation and imaginative escape.

In addition to over five hundred pieces created by Burton himself, the exhibition includes work by a number of his important collaborators: the studios of Mackinnon and Saunders in Cheshire, England; Carlos Grangel in Barcelona; the Chiodo Brothers and Gentle Giant, both based in Burbank, California; his earliest professional collaborators, Rick Heinrichs and Joe Ranft; costume designer Colleen Atwood; concept artists Kelly Asbury, Chris Baker, Bill Boes, Mauro Borrelli, Kendal Cronkhite, Michael Jackson, Shane Mahan, John Puglisi, John Rosengrant, Felipe Sanchez, Ian Stephenson, Deane Taylor, Christopher Ure, and Simón Vladimir Varela; character designers and fabricators Colin Batty and Bonita DeCarlo; prop artists David Balfour and Doug Brode; animator Barry Purves; and directors Mike Johnson and Henry Selick.

As they did with *Pixar: 20 Years of Animation* in 2005, Ron Magliozzi, Assistant Curator, and Jenny He, Curatorial Assistant in the Museum's Department of Film, have demonstrated their skill in the organization of heretofore unexhibited material. Their project was supported by Rajendra Roy, The Celeste Bartos Chief Curator of Film. An exhibition on this scale, with its accompanying film series, would not be possible without the enthusiastic cooperation of our studio and private lenders, Warner Bros., Disney, Twentieth Century Fox, Sony, Paramount, Karen Winston, Ron Magid, and the very generous financial support of visionary cable channel Syfy. To them all we express our sincere thanks.

Glenn D. Lowry
Director, The Museum of Modern Art

TIM BURTON:
EXERCISING THE IMAGINATION

For Tim Burton, drawing is exercise for a restless imagination.

It is a way to occupy his hands when they are not otherwise engaged directing or producing movies. What began as an outlet for the nervous energy he felt growing up in Burbank, California, soon led to stop-motion animated films staged with toy action figures and school friends in neighborhood backyards. In spite of his claims that he was an inarticulate youth who felt alienated from his suburban environment, Burton's point of view has always been humorous and high-spirited.[1] His earliest drawings are comic, borrowing the style of cartoons studiously clipped from periodicals, and his first films, with parts for himself as the Doctor of Doom and Rigger T. Mortis, celebrated misunderstood, evil masterminds typical of the movies that offered him the different kind of role models and the colorful life he craved. By the age of eighteen, when Burton enrolled in the California Institute of the Arts (CalArts), he was already using some of the most disposable forms of American pop culture—television cartoons, B movies, comic strips, advertising, toys—to fashion the alternative self-image that would make him a brand name by the time *Tim Burton's The Nightmare Before Christmas,* his sixth feature, was released in 1993.[2]

Burton made much of his disaffected youth in Burbank as muse for his early work. The settings for his shorts *Vincent* (1982) and *Frankenweenie* (1984), and the frenzied finale of *Pee-wee's Big Adventure* (1985), the pastel suburbia of *Edward Scissorhands* (1990), and the punishing small-town dystopia of *Beetlejuice* (1988) all reflect the Hollywood suburb, which is also home to Warner Bros. and Disney, the very studios for whom he would later work. Even the clash of Halloween and

Christmas hometowns triggered by the angst-ridden Jack Skellington in *Nightmare* has autobiographical implications as a Burbank escape fantasy.[3] Although Burton has made a new life for himself as an expatriate in London, England, and clearly savors his geographical distance from Hollywood, as an artist he has always nurtured an engagement with his past. He is attached to the playful aesthetics of drawing and animation, and to tools associated with childhood, such as crayons and colored pencils, because they connect him with pleasures of the imagination that he learned to value in adolescence and continue to inform his work as an adult. Indeed, the intercourse between childhood and adulthood is a consistent subtext throughout Burton's oeuvre, and explains his attraction to fairy tales, children's literature, gothic horror, and science fiction as genres through which to explore this most personal and universal theme. Burton's cross-generational perspective, configuring youthful enthusiasm and sentiment with adult libido, gives his work its distinctive character, and may explain his appeal to both a mass audience and a cult following.

Timothy Walter Burton was born on August 25, 1958. By his own account, he survived a benignly dysfunctional family consisting of two parents and a younger brother. His father, with whom he remained permanently at odds, worked in athletics for the Burbank Parks and Recreation Department, while his mother ran a gift shop named Cat's Plus. He describes himself then as both an introvert and a practical joker. There were incidents of being forced to hibernate in his room at home, and eventually he moved in with his grandmother. He wasn't much of a reader, and even avoided comic books in part because they contained too many words. Drawing and visual media were his pain-relievers of choice.

Burton's keepsakes and scrapbooks from the period attest to his voracious consumption of pop culture. He collected greeting cards, made lists of the horror and science-fiction films that teased his imagination, sketched his favorite star, Vincent Price, and created posters for a horror-film series sponsored by the Police Youth Band. Amid this memorabilia, the most illuminating items may be the comics culled from newspapers and magazines, with illustrations by mainstream cartoonists such as Henry Syverson (*Saturday Evening Post*), who observed the battle of the sexes with wry wit; Angelo Torres (*Mad Magazine*), the zany cultural caricaturist; and Gahan Wilson (*National Lampoon*), the mordant adult cartoonist and follower of H. P. Lovecraft.[4] Burton's efforts to emulate their drawing styles were fleeting, but their skewed view of American society had a lasting influence on his sensibility. Homework assignments, too, proved an apt way for him to pursue his pop interests. A 1975 high school English paper titled "Humor in America" inventoried examples of satire, parody, and jokes found in print, TV, movies, advertising, and everyday conversation.

Ironically, it was the Burbank town fathers—who steadfastly maintained the ordinary way of life Burton rebelled against— who first rewarded his precocious talent with public recognition. In 1976 he won a day at the fire station for his contribution to a fire-prevention campaign, and a year later his picture and a drawing he'd made in support of the football team appeared on the cover of the *Burbank City Employee Newsletter*. As winner of a "Beautify Burbank" contest sponsored by the Chamber of Commerce, he saw his cartoon *Crush Litter* displayed on the sides of city garbage trucks. Then at eighteen, Burton won a scholarship to attend CalArts, a fine arts school founded by Walt and Roy Disney to encourage the joint study of the visual and performing arts in a

Untitled (Boy Series)
1995. Pastel, watercolor, and acrylic on paper, 17 × 14" (43.2 × 35.6 cm). Private collection

supportive workshop environment. That same year, Walt Disney Productions politely rejected a children's book he had written and fully illustrated, *The Giant Zlig*, because it was "too derivative of the Seuss works to be marketable."[5] (The animated version of Dr. Seuss's *How the Grinch Stole Christmas* [1957], adapted for television in 1966 by legendary Warner Bros. animator Chuck Jones and narrated by Boris Karloff, was a noteworthy early influence on Burton.)

At CalArts, Burton's education as a professional artist exposed him to traditional art history and theory. In his notebook he dutifully recorded such basic lessons as Realism versus Romanticism in the work of Courbet and Goya, and he took away an appreciation of Post-Impressionism: "If I look at certain Van Gogh paintings, they're not real, but they capture such an energy that makes it real."[6] His classroom sketchbooks contain still-life drawings of armor and fruit, typical "art school" studies of human and animal musculature, and formal exercises in cartooning and animation. The unique environment of CalArts offered him ample opportunity for exploration and self-discovery. As a prospective animator he was allowed to indulge his penchant for delinquent doodling and creature making, the standard stuff of adolescent male fantasy, alternating academic nudes with bizarre aliens, humanoid insects, and battling dinosaurs. His was the kind of raw talent the Disney instructors expected could be trained to serve the company. His graduate project, a four-minute animated film titled *The Stalk of the Celery Monster* (1979), in which a mad doctor's torture chamber is revealed to be a dentist's office, is a whimsical sketchbook illustration brought to life, and demonstrated Burton's peculiar taste for merging the gothic with the everyday.

In 1979 Burton began a four-year apprenticeship with the Disney studio during which he worked as an in-betweener, assistant animator, and concept artist.[7]

His first assignment was on the feature *The Fox and the Hound* (1981), a project initiated by Frank Thomas and Ollie Johnston, the last of the studio's renowned masters of traditional animation known as the "Nine Old Men."[8] Temperamentally unsuited to the film's pastoral sentiment and uninspiring characters—Burton was charged with animating the hero's bland love interest—he felt imprisoned and depressed. *The Black Cauldron* (1985), a medieval fantasy about a magical device that produces armies of the undead, was more to his liking. Inspired by the notion of conflating human and mechanical reproduction, he produced his first important body of professional work with a series of satiric killing machines, monstrous baby incubators that use infants as ammunition, and other radically un-Disney-like, anthropomorphic creatures. None of his nearly two-hundred drawings were used for the finished film.

Although Burton found life as a studio contract artist all but unbearable, he responded with an outpouring of creativity, just as he had when faced with the frustrating circumstances of his childhood. The early 1980s, in the years leading up to his first feature, *Pee-wee*, was a remarkably rich period. Building on his education and apprenticeship, Burton now developed an aesthetic foundation that would serve as an imaginative resource for the studio films and other independent projects that followed. Signature themes and key stylistic traits, such as creature-based notions of character, the use of masks, and body modification, began to emerge. His interest in the theme of adolescent and adult opposition in particular came to bear on his choice of subject matter, and how he adapted this material for movies.

During this time he produced an impressive number of innovative and fresh story ideas intended for animated films, a body of work that still feels ripe with imagination. To familiar adolescent subjects he brought edgy sophistication: for Toys (1980), a jack-in-the box, wind-ups, and baby doll carriages serve as innocent decoys for lethal military weaponry; his character studies for Pirates (1980) manipulate human bodies to the point of structural abstraction; and for the sci-fi *Alien* (1983), he plays with black light and a pastel palette to picture surreal outer-space life-forms. Some of his unrealized projects were not developed much beyond their humorous premises, such as *Little Dead Riding Hood* (1981), a fractured fairy tale that shifts the balance of power in favor of its skeletal heroine, or *Romeo and Juliet* (1981–84), which re-imagines Shakespeare as a tragic romance between a land mass and an ocean mass. *Dream Factory* (1983), a satire of the Hollywood studio system, has traces of a narrative involving an abused stunt dummy and a full cast of characters including a scriptwriting dinosaur, a toad director, an imprisoned animator, and an audience of talking theater seats. A second children's book, *Numbers* (1982), that also failed to find a publisher, pictures the numerals one to ten as unnatural animal and insect creatures engaged in the *scary* antics of eating, sport, and courtship.

Of the projects Burton developed during this creatively fertile time, *Nightmare* is the best known. But two others left behind, *Trick or Treat* (1980) and *True Love* (1981–1983), prefigure much of his later work. It is not difficult to appreciate how a story of isolated suburban kids discovering a world of grotesque creatures, or another about two sensation-starved boys taking on the shapes of monstrous warring toys, would have resonated with Burton. Both deal with the awakening of the imagination and the transformative nature of experience, and trade in notions and motifs—innocent youth and adult duplicity, the joy of creation, anthropomorphism, masks, armor, and the cartooning of character psychology—that would find expression in the live-action films that were to come. Throughout some one-hundred-eighty engaging studies for *Trick or Treat*, the evolution of Burton's draftsmanship is revealed. In a few drawings, he mimics the styles of Maurice Sendak, Charles Addams, and Edward Gorey before finding his own voice with a menagerie of pierced, stitched, and self-abused creatures that anticipate *Tragic Toys for Girls and Boys*, the collectible figures he created for Dark Horse Comics in 2003.

From the start of his professional career in 1979, aided by fellow CalArts graduate Rick Heinrichs, his most sympathetic and important early collaborator, Burton had been making a case for the practice of stop-motion animation to art-school colleagues and studio executives.[9] To this end Heinrichs brought Burton's drawings for *Trick or Treat, True Love, Dream Factory, Hansel and Gretel* (1983), *Vincent*, and *Nightmare* to life as sculpted, three-dimensional maquettes. In the space of two years their ambitious proposals and growing reputations as singular talents led to Burton's first professional jobs as a film director when Disney agreed to fund the stop-motion *Vincent*, the live-action *Frankenweenie*, and his Japanese cast version of *Hansel and Gretel* for broadcast on their fledgling cable channel. Diligently, in over fourteen-hundred drawings, Burton fully storyboarded all three projects, a task he would later execute only for key sequences of *Pee-wee* and *Nightmare* as the scale of his projects grew.

Untitled (Miscellaneous)
1980. Ink, watercolor, and colored pencil on paper.
9 × 8" (22.9 × 20.3 cm). Private collection

While Burton struggled to find a place within an industry that catered to the broadest possible audience, he cultivated his private ambitions to make art, turning to drawing, painting, photography, and writing with increasing seriousness. The earliest of this personal work, created between 1980 and 1986, are over fifty cartoons done in pencil on animation registration paper (a medium that suggests they came about as on-the-job diversion). Resembling the kind of roguish observational humor he had clipped from magazines as a child, the cartoons escalate in edgy charm from whimsical wordplay ("Little Mary Cemetery") to the pun inspired ("mental floss") and scatological ("Why You Shouldn't Shoot a Constipated Poodle"). They demonstrate a gift for comedy and storytelling in miniature that tends to be overshadowed by the Gothic character and scale of visual effects in Burton's films. The doodles, sketches, notions ("Ventriloquism in the Days of Shakespeare") and fragments of narrative ("there was a young man everyone thought was quite handsome, so he tied up his face, and he held it for ransom") that filled Burton's desk blotters and notebooks would fuel later projects. For example, the films *Vincent* and *Nightmare* first took shape as poetry, and *The Melancholy Death of Oyster Boy and Other Stories* (1997), an illustrated book of verse on childhood comprising twenty-three mordant vignettes, and *The World of Stainboy*, a six-part cartoon series for the Web featuring a biohazard superhero, grew from Burton's sketchbook inspiration.

Following the cartoons were over three-hundred more-focused studies of women, men, and couples rendered in ink, watercolor, and paint from the late 1980s. (They could hardly be described as *more formal* because Burton continued to use casual and provocative surfaces like pocket note pads, cocktail napkins, and contraceptive cases.) With these Burton explored the excesses of perspective and proportion, occasionally producing a kind of Pop Cubism that was as much a testament to the classic animation practice of "squash and stretch" as it was a riff on Picasso.[10] Coming from a time in his twenties when he felt estranged from the world at large, the work has an outsider's point of view: unsentimental, delightfully cynical, and rife with unspent sexual energy. Caricaturing the ages of man, self-inflated personalities, heterosexual mating rituals, and, in a rare instance an actual celebrity, President Reagan, the drawings have an air of social commentary. Burton is an engaged reader of daily newspapers, and although few would likely describe him as a political filmmaker, a critique of community and mistrust of social relationships underscore his work. The critical spirit of his drawings from this period is translated to film in *Mars Attacks!* (1996), when an army of giggling Martians systematically destroys the incompetent political, military, media, and business elite of the United States.[11]

Though his isolated art practice and sympathy for social outcasts suggests he had a loner mentality, Burton was not alone in his eager absorption of "low" culture. The evolution of the Pop Surrealist phenomenon (also known as "Lowbrow Art") coincides with the forty-year period of Burton's childhood and professional career and is an apt reference point.[12] Pop Surrealism took root in Southern California in the late 1960s when a diverse, loose-knit group of illustrators and painters turned away from dominant traditions of abstract and conceptual art in favor of representational forms of expression. Inspired by the most accessible and amusing kinds of "lowbrow" popular culture—custom cars, tattoo art, pinups, comics, toys, monster and sci-fi movies, animation, and alternative music—painters such as Robert Williams laid the foundation for a new kind of contemporary art that was an alternative to the usual museum fare. This was the same delightfully lurid ethos that Burton had begun exploring on his own as an adolescent, and much that is distinctive in his films and personal projects, and easily recognized in his paintings, like *Blue Girl with Wine* (c. 1997), and his oversize Polaroid photographs (1992–1999) shares this colorful, hip outsider perspective.

Burton could not help but be aware of LA's burgeoning artistic scene, and certain Pop Surrealist motifs being explored at the time found their way into his work. He enjoyed the musical cabaret of LA performance artists the Mystic Knights of the Oingo Boingo, from whom he eventually took away Danny Elfman, who would become his longtime music collaborator.[13] The flow of fluids used throughout his films, be it the rivers of chocolate in *Charlie and the Chocolate Factory* (2005) or the gushing blood in *Sweeney Todd: The Demon Barber of Fleet Street* (2007), the candy cream of *Hansel and Gretel* or the bile of "The Jar" (1986), may be interpreted as a nod to avant-garde performance art.[14] The oversize eyes that stare from Robert Williams's seminal Pop Surrealist painting *In the Land of Retinal Delights* (1968) and move through performances by the Residents, in their

Untitled (Miscellaneous)
c. 1990–93. Ink and watercolor on paper, 11 × 9″
(27.9 × 22.9 cm). Private collection

iconic eyeball-head masks, imply voyeuristic compulsion.[15] In this regard, Burton's most identifiably Pop Surrealist creations may be the illustrated *Oyster Boy* and *Stainboy* stories in which the punctured, empty eye sockets of abused children serve as windows onto tortured souls and a response to a troubling world of sensation without feeling. It is not surprising that Burton and Pop Surrealist artist Mark Ryden were equally entranced by the preternaturally large, round eyes and doll-like perfection of actress Christina Ricci, who was the subject of Ryden's 1998 painting *Christina* and the female lead of Burton's *Sleepy Hollow*.[16]

In *Doctor of Doom*, the eponymous character, performed by a teenaged Tim Burton, instructs the monster he's created to "destroy all beauty," and Burton has endeavored ever since to come up with new models for the beautiful. Skeletons, severed heads, and bodies and eyes that are stitched and pierced are recurring emblems whose twofold effect is to skewer conformist attitudes and affirm alternative ways of life.[17] Indeed, disfiguring the body allows Burton to deliver metaphors of social dysfunction and psychological disintegration with sensual wit. Severed heads, for example, are featured players in *Sleepy Hollow* and serve as two of the romantic leads in *Mars*. (Burton himself appears as one on a surfboard and a buffet table in his student film *Luau* [1980].) He readily credits his affection for the grotesque to horror films and *Day of the Dead* rituals, the latter of which he demonstrates when he roasts the United States Congress into skeletal Red Hots in *Mars Attacks!* thereby invoking the tradition of editorializing Mexican *calaveras*.[18] Meanwhile the skeletons of *Trick or Treat, Nightmare, Tim Burton's Corpse Bride* (2005), and the 2006 music video for "Bones,"[19] exhibit a festive plasticity that owes more to the racy, improvisatory style of Fleischer Studio animation.[20] But physical mutilation is more than a form of satire for

Burton: with *Nightmare*'s stitched Sally, his tattooed Blue Girls, and the pierced Pin Cushion Queen and Voodoo Girl of *Oyster Boy*, he also revels in the erotic, self-determining culture of bod-mod punk body art.

In line with the figurative nature of Pop Surrealism, Burton delights in the exaggerated manipulation of the body. Japanese Transformer toys were an important early influence and his drawings often picture anthropomorphic creatures—part man, animal, and machine—in the grip of some transformative emotion. His attention to the creature-like qualities of his characters is a way for him to access their humanity: the cartoon concept art for Batman and the Joker emphasizes their damaged psyches; the drawings of Edward Scissorhands's sinister bondage gear and Jack Skellington's freakish emaciation translates to their soulfulness on screen. The masks and armor worn by his characters are yet another manifestation of the *creatures* lurking within, as demonstrated by the heavy expressionistic gear of the *Batman* films, *Planet of the Apes* (2001), *Sleepy Hollow*, and *Scissorhands*, and by the more transparent "mask" and "armor" represented by Johnny Depp's forced grin and shocking pink sweater in the California Gothic *Ed Wood* (1994). In the process of conceiving character, Burton regularly returns to cartooning. When he jokes that many of his drawings look the same, he refers to the basic triangular forms he uses when inventing lead characters such as Vincent, Scissorhands, and Sweeney Todd, and the circular shapes that define Oyster Boy and Stainboy.[21] Examining his visual shorthand of pointed and rounded faces and bodies, it becomes clear that Burton's triangles and circles stand for *trouble* and *loss*.

The carnivalesque—a liberating mix of comedy and the grotesque in defiance of the status quo—is a significant component of Burton's work, where it is often visualized as an actual experience of circus or fairground entertainment.[22] Carnival-inspired surrealism infuses the drama and comedy of the *Batman* films, *Pee-wee*, *Beetlejuice*, *Mars*, *Big Fish* (2003), and *Charlie* as well as the biographical *Ed Wood*. The figures of clowns, puppets, pumpkins, and scarecrows, and the visual repetition of stripes, question marks, and primary colors that appear throughout his work are manifestations of his carnivalesque sensibility. For Burton, a bright palette is typically the sign of an unnerving, often sinister, attraction. Anything with the power to capture the imagination may corrupt the unwary: a parade ends in mass destruction (*Batman*), a visit to a candy factory leads to physical abuse (*Charlie*), and considering that Santa Claus himself is really just another colorful clown, even the Christmas holiday is suspect (*Nightmare*).

Burton's predatory clowns and other disquieting, misunderstood creatures point to core themes of human duplicity and the opposing, fretting ages of man.[23] The scenes of encounter between adolescence and adulthood that he stages time and again—via parent-child conversations and youthful challenges to authority—speak to his feelings about artistic imagination and the limitations of circumstance.[24] In the end, creativity is the saving grace of Tim Burton's heroes, whether they appear on paper as many-limbed, multitasking monsters, or on screen as woebegone humans sculpting shrubs and ice, inventing tall tales, directing exploitation films, slitting throats, or surviving Wonderland. Their example of imaginative activity, as a response to conditions of disconnection and isolation, is the overarching message of Burton's work.

Notes

1 Tim Burton, interview by Melvyn Bragg, *The South Bank Show*, ITV, January 20, 2008.
2 As a name-above-the-title auteur, Burton might usefully be compared to artists like Federico Fellini, a filmmaker who drew and painted constantly on the pages of a private dream diary, or Andy Warhol, who made the transition from world-renowned Pop artist to cult filmmaker.
3 In the late 1980s Burton wanted to adapt Edgar Allan Poe's *The Fall of the House of*

Usher as a comedy set in Burbank, and even commissioned screenwriter Jonathan Gems to write the screenplay. Anthony C. Ferrante, "Hidden Gems," in *Tim Burton: A Child's Garden of Nightmares*, 129.
4 Burton's early scrapbooks also contain the syndicated comic strips *B.C.* (1958–2007), a series about cavemen by Johnny Hart (1931–2007), and *Tumbleweeds* (1965–2007), a Western series by Tom K. Ryan (b. 1926). H.P. Lovecraft (1890–1937) was an American

writer of fantasy, horror, and science fiction.
5 Theodor Seuss Geisel (1904–1991), an American writer and cartoonist who published under the pen name "Dr. Seuss," was the author of very popular children's books written in rhymed verse such as *The Cat in the Hat* (1957) and *Green Eggs and Ham* (1960).
6 Tim Burton, *Burton on Burton*, 175 and interview by Bragg, *The South Bank Show*: Bragg: "The two painters you've spoken about are Van Gogh and Francis Bacon. What

is it about them that attracts you particularly?" Burton: "I remember when I first saw paintings in person, the energy that was captured…it was electric to me. I'd never really experienced that before, especially the landscapes…that were really amazing…"

7 An in-betweener produces the series of drawings that link previously completed key poses done by senior animators. It is an entry-level position in an animation department.

8 Frank Thomas (1912–2004) and Ollie Johnston (1912–2008) were the last of the "Nine Old Men," Disney's core animators who determined the studio's animation style from the late 1930s through the 1980s. The hand-drawn, two-dimensional animation they practiced was overshadowed by Pixar's computer-generated *Toy Story* (1995) and the stop-motion aesthetic of *Nightmare*.

9 In the early 1970s, inspired by the stop-motion model animation of producer and special-effects creator Ray Harryhausen (b. 1920) in such films as *Jason and the Argonauts* (1963), Burton staged an amateur short, *The Island of Dr. Agor* (1971), using cavemen action figures.

10 "Squash and stretch" is a key principle of traditional 2-D cel animation. Animators use "squash and stretch" for added comedic effect, and to give drawn objects an illusion of dimension and volume.

11 Burton had originally intended the Martian destruction to be global, but due to budget limitations, he could only afford to destroy the Eiffel Tower, Big Ben, the Easter Island statues, and the Taj Mahal. Anthony C. Ferrante, "Hidden Gems," in *Tim Burton: A Child's Garden of Nightmares*, 129.

12 Pop Surrealism, alternately known as "Lowbrow Art," has been described as more of a zeitgeist than a movement. According to Christopher Knight ("The New Pop is Everywhere You Look," *LA Times*, December 24, 2006), it represents "the spirit of the 21st Century." Some two-hundred artists have exhibited or been anthologized under this rubric, including Robert Williams (widely acknowledged as the movement's father), Gary Baseman, Ron English, Camille Rose Garcia, Liz McGrath, Scott Musgrove, Gary Panter, Mark Ryden, and Todd Schorr. *Juxtapoz Art & Culture Magazine* has provided the most comprehensive record of Pop Surrealism since the magazine was founded in 1994.

13 Richard Elfman founded the Mystic Knights of the Oingo Boingo in 1972, and was soon joined by his brother Danny. The feature film *Forbidden Zone* (Richard Elfman and Matthew Wright, 1980) documents the Mystic Knights' unique style of performance, which featured musicians dressed as skeletons and clowns as well as surrealist set design that included severed heads and anthropomorphic elements. The troupe lasted until 1980 when it changed format and became the New Wave rock group Oingo Boingo, releasing the relevantly themed album *Dead Man's Party* in 1985.

14 "The Jar," an episode of the *Alfred Hitchcock Presents* television series originally broadcast on April 6, 1986, concerns an uninspired Conceptual artist whose acquisition of a jar containing a gelatinous subhuman life form leads to a struggle with his bilious wife that ends in butchery and some gruesome modern art.

15 The eyeball-head masks worn by the Residents were adapted for the "Monster in the Playhouse" episode (1986) of *Pee-wee's Playhouse* (1986–1990), a children's Saturday morning television program inspired by the success of Burton's 1985 theatrical feature. Artist Gary Panter also worked on the TV series as production designer. It is interesting to note that Matt Groening (*Life in Hell*, *The Simpsons*) is the other artist with links to Pop Surrealism whose film and television work, like Burton's, has enjoyed outstanding international success.

16 See also Mark Ryden's painting *The Apology* (2006) and his other works featuring wide-eyed, porcelain-skin subjects.

17 Images of skeletons, severed heads, and stitched-up bodies and eyes have also been favored by the Pop Surrealists as well as the younger generation of Goth-inspired artists who followed after 2000, as documented in *Hell Bound: New Gothic Art*.

18 *El Día de los Muertos* or All Saints Day is a Mexican holiday dedicated to the remembrance of family and friends who have died. Rituals involve skulls and skeleton figures known as *calaveras*, masks, graveyard decoration, and offerings of toys, candy, and chocolate for the deceased. In the work of illustrators like José Guadalupe Posada (1852–1913), *calaveras* were used for the purposes of social and political commentary.

19 The song "Bones" by the Las Vegas–based rock band The Killers, from their album *Sam's Town* (2006), was released as a single on November 27, 2006. Burton filmed the band when they performed in Los Angeles on August 17 and 18 to make the video, which is set in a drive-in movie theater, a beach, and desert locations.

20 Fleischer Studios, Inc., 1921–1942, was an East Coast company based in New York City and a major Disney rival. Its cartoon stars included Betty Boop, Popeye, Superman, and Koko the Clown. The surreal style and vulgar humanity of its early 1930s shorts influenced a number of underground comix and Lowbrow artists. Danny Elfman brought his affection for Fleischer's Cab Calloway shorts—*Minnie the Moocher* (1932), *Snow White* (1933), and *The Old Man of the Mountain* (1933)—to bear on Burton's work, most obviously in *Corpse Bride*.

21 Tim Burton, Commentary Disc 1, Special Features: *Burton + Depp + Carter = Todd*, in *Sweeney Todd: The Demon Barber of Fleet Street* (2-Disc Special Collector's Edition), DVD, 2008, and interview by Bragg, *The South Bank Show*: "I have a fairly limited sort of sketching style, so characters always kind of look the same, things always look… a bit similar."

22 The *carnivalesque* and the *grotesque body* were terms coined by Russian literary critic Mikhail Bakhtin (1895–1975). Notions of carnival as a form of liberation from conservative hegemonies have been traced to the work of writers Rabelais and Cervantes, and in the broader history of art to artists such as Hieronymus Bosch, Louise Bourgeois, Pieter Bruegel, James Ensor, Francisco Goya, Red Grooms, and George Grosz, and performance artists like Leigh Bowery and Paul McCarthy, among others.

Knowing that "the carnivalesque has acted as a corrective to each successive hegemony in the visual arts" (Hyman, "A Carnival Sense of the World," *Carnivalesque*, 72) may help us to appreciate the spirit in which Burton reacted against the aesthetic of the "Nine Old Men" which dominated the animated film industry for most of the twentieth century.

23 Evil clowns are familiar characters in comic books (*Batman* [1940–], *Insane Clown Posse* [2000–2001]) and films (*Killer Klowns from Outer Space* [1988], *Clownhouse* [1989], Stephen King's *IT* [1990], *Spawn* [1997]). Burton's research collection contains an image of serial killer John Wayne Gacy (1924–1994) in the clown makeup he wore as an entertainer at children's parties.

24 A noteworthy historical image of the carnivalesque that resonates with this theme in Burton's work appears on an anonymous broadsheet published in Belfast in 1840. Titled *The Miller's Man: Grinding Old People Young*, it pictures a line of elderly men and women climbing up a ladder, tumbling into one end of a large meat grinder, and coming out the other end as children. *Carnivalesque*, 6.

Jenny He

AN AUTEUR FOR ALL AGES

A director of fables, fairy tales, and fantasies, with an aesthetic that incorporates the Gothic, the Grand Guignol, and German Expressionism, Tim Burton is an uncompromised visionary – a modern auteur.[1]

His body of films thus far, fourteen features[2] released over the past two and a half decades, has resulted in a style so distinctive that it is referred to in the vernacular as "Burtonesque."

This trademark results from his particular choice of telling stories chiefly through striking visuals and indelible characters who personify the themes that recur and reverberate throughout all of his works—primarily the isolation of being disconnected from the world at large and the search for true identity. Edward Scissorhands (*Edward Scissorhands*, 1990), incapable of directly touching others with his razor-sharp fingers, is the physical manifestation of isolation. Batman, Catwoman, and the Penguin (*Batman Returns*, 1992) battle not only with each other but with the fact that they must maintain dual identities. Jack Skellington (*Tim Burton's The Nightmare Before Christmas*, 1993), discontented with the monotony of success at being the "Pumpkin King" of "Halloween Town," attempts a new role: "Sandy Claws." Leo Davidson (*Planet of the Apes*, 2001) finds himself as the lone evolutionarily superior human in a simian world. Edward Bloom (*Big Fish*, 2003) retreats into telling tall tales about his youth, which alienates him from his son. "I'm amazed at people…

who can go from genre to genre, and every movie seems different," Burton has said in explanation of his consistent approach. "I need some sort of connection."[3]

Burton established himself as a director with an unusual personal vision in his first feature, *Pee-wee's Big Adventure* (1985). The plot hinges on Pee-wee's search for his missing bicycle, a scenario that is more or less an excuse to indulge in whimsical set pieces and extravagant sight gags. His encounter with a spectral trucker is an opportunity for "eye-popping" stop-motion effects. The climactic ride through the Warner Bros. back lot is a montage of zany fun as Pee-wee and his beloved bike zoom through a beach blanket bingo set, the North Pole, Godzilla's rampage, a Twisted Sister music video, and Tarzan's jungle. Like the elaborate Rube Goldberg–esque contraption (a familiar Burton motif) that facilitates Pee-wee's morning routine, the simple plots of Burton's films unfold in visually complex ways. His willingness to dive wholeheartedly into the sensual and ridiculous may mean that critics occasionally dismiss Burton's films as mere visual confections, but he has a ready rebuttal, voiced through a character in one of his most poignant films. As Charlie Bucket sagely remarks in *Charlie and the Chocolate Factory* (2005): "Candy doesn't have to have a point. That's why it's candy."

The pleasurable aspect of Burton's fantastic and strange films invites audiences to sense them on an emotional level rather than rationally digest them. Favoring instinct and intuition versus strictly following words on a page, Burton moved away from rigid storyboarding as early as 1988, when he made *Beetlejuice*.[4] The director values the immediacy and intimacy of working out scenes with actors on set, and in doing so, he has developed his own way of communicating with actors. Johnny Depp—one of Burton's most frequent collaborators— recalled of *Edward Scissorhands*: "Tim showed me several drawings of his Edward. I'd read the script, of course, but Tim's drawings said everything. I instantly fell for the character—he made his way into my body."[5]

Although Burton's films can be enjoyed without need for intellectual dissection, their foundations are nonetheless deeply rooted in consistent visuals, characters, and themes that evolve and comment on each other throughout his work. Upon examination, there exists a particular methodology consisting of certain key components—the things that make a Tim Burton film a Tim Burton film.

Without a doubt, Burton's films are identifiable by virtue of the imaginative universes that they conjure. Sumptuous production design sprouts seemingly from a stream of unmitigated inventive consciousness. Settings are not limited by the parameters, logic, and physics of reality, operating instead by rationales of Burton's own creation. In *Beetlejuice*, the metamorphosis of the Maitlands' house reflects the movie's transcendence into different levels of unreality.[6] The house starts as a typical New England home. As fantastic elements emerge from the underworld through the conduit of Beetlejuice, the

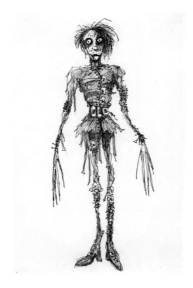

Untitled (*Edward Scissorhands*)
1990. Ink on paper, 8 × 5" (20.3 × 12.7 cm).
Private collection

abode becomes a postmodern funhouse, growing more and more gaudy and grotesque as the movie progresses. Bo Welch, the film's production designer, describes it as "a hierarchy of reality that leads you into unreality. Tim would encourage me to push that border. I'd go a certain distance, and he'd say, 'Let's go further,' and I'd go 'Arrghhh!' and then be thrilled when we did it."[7] Of the making of *Batman* (1989), production designer Anton Furst notes, "I don't believe in cinema verité. You should create your own reality. We ended up with this rather interesting idea of canyons, with structures cantilevered forward and bridges over them. We even took things like prison architecture and stretched it into skyscrapers."[8] Burton's Gotham City is deliberately unrecognizable to the inhabitants of any actual city in the world.

Even in films set in real-life locations, such as *Sleepy Hollow* (1999), Burton suggests worlds of "otherness." Working with production designer Rick Heinrichs, who has collaborated with the director on numerous projects, they took liberties with the Dutch colonial setting of 1799 upstate New York and made their own expressionistic Sleepy Hollow in Lime Tree Valley, England—a form of "stylized naturalism." Instead of using the existing nature in the countryside, they built their own forest, which held as its centerpiece the "tree of the dead," (Heinrichs describes it as "agony captured in wood sculpture"[9]), the literal gateway between earth and the beyond.

In addition to the "unreal" aspect of the filmic locations, there is often an environmental and atmospheric dichotomy. Two distinct worlds exist simultaneously—whether in the mind only or in an alternate reality such as the netherworld—and only a few select characters traverse between the two. The "normal" world is exposed as claustrophobic and suffocating while the "topsy-turvy" world is

Paul Reubens as Pee-wee in *Pee-wee's Big Adventure*
1985. 35mm film, color, sound, 90 minutes

Johnny Depp as Ichabod Crane in *Sleepy Hollow*
1999. 35mm film, color, sound, 105 minutes

Alison Lohman as Sandra Templeton and
Ewan McGregor as Edward Bloom in *Big Fish*
2003. 35mm film, color, sound,125 minutes

Johnny Depp as Ed Wood and
Martin Landau as Bela Lugosi in *Ed Wood*
1994. 35mm film, black and white, sound,127 minutes

colorful, imaginative, and revelatory, and often turns out to be more logical.

In *Big Fish*, the present is monochromatic, in contrast with the colorful flashbacks of Edward Bloom's life: Bloom in a blue suit seducing his future wife while sitting in a field of yellow daffodils; his visit to the town of Spectre, a vision in green; his stint working for the circus, a panoply of red-hued costumes and decorations. In *Tim Burton's Corpse Bride* (2005), the living trudge along in muted tones of gray and mauve while the underworld is alive with a palette of vibrant purples, greens, and blues. In *Charlie and the Chocolate Factory*, London life is depicted in a haze of leached-out hues (reminiscent of the color palette of Terence Davies's films portraying the weary working class and their daily routines) while the polychromatic interior of the chocolate factory vibrates with energy and effervescence.

But Burton's films are not identifiable only from their visual cues. Looked at as a whole, at their core, his movies also address the duality of childhood and adulthood. Shuttling between the fancies, freedoms, and unbridled imaginative possibilities of youth and the knowing, world-weary, and saturnine attitudes that come with age, Burton's films operate on multiple layers. They appeal to children, but contain a sensibility only adults can truly grasp: *Beetlejuice* is replete with sophomoric delights such as the shrunken heads and flattened corpses that occupy the director's cynical version of hell as a bureaucratic waiting room where red tape abounds. A reviewer of the movie attributed to Burton both the "imagination of a demonic nine-year-old" and of making the "kind of maniacal concoction only an adult could fully appreciate."[10]

The presence of comedy amid the macabre, another major component in all of Burton's films, offsets lascivious characters and gore-filled and graphic action. The licentious sexuality of lechers such as Beetlejuice (*Beetlejuice*), the Penguin (*Batman Returns*), and

Untitled (*Beetlejuice*)
1988. Ink and colored pencil on paper, 9 × 12"
(22.9 × 30.5 cm). Private collection

Judge Turpin (*Sweeney Todd: The Demon Barber of Fleet Street*, 2007), is never explicit, and the double entendres issuing from their leering countenances are more hilarious than offensive. Likewise, the violence in Burton's films is more often cartoonish and unrealistic than disturbing. When humans are incinerated by ray guns in *Mars Attacks!* (1996), their charred skeletons are left bright red and green. The demise of the First Lady in that film comes from a falling chandelier, and it is almost expected that an enormously long tongue would unfurl and roll out of her head à la a Warner Bros. cartoon. Severed heads in *Sleepy Hollow* spin in place for a while on the necks from which they were recently detached, while blood spurts in geysers and bodies drop with exaggerated thuds down a long chute with animated effect in *Sweeney Todd*. Burton's playful humor counterbalances the shocking and frees the audience to revel in the grotesque.

While Burton's unique visuals and specific themes contribute to his auteur aesthetic and style, the linchpin of Burton's work is his embrace of character. Despite the fact that the majority of his films become blockbusters,[11] Burton's projects are all intimate affairs, inhabited by elaborately developed characters who provide the emotional depth to the films. Burton has said of this motivation, "I love extreme characters who totally believe themselves."[12]

Many of Burton's characters are specific archetypes that Burton has developed and cultivated over the years, and that help to define his personal vision. Two significant recurring archetypes are the flawed father and the misunderstood outcast. Both mean well but ultimately disappoint. Portrayed with reverence both narratively and stylistically, the flawed father often manifests as intangible: he is either projected on film or appears in flashbacks, dreams, and hallucinations—techniques that communicate the detached and distant nature of the character. In addition, the death of the flawed father is often a key moment in the story. His fleeting existence almost belies his significance as the one who defines the misunderstood outcast's primary motivations.

In *Ed Wood* (1994), for example, the character of Bela Lugosi (Martin Landau) is the embodiment of the flawed father. He and Ed Wood (Johnny Depp) have a codependent, surrogate-father/son relationship; true to form, Lugosi comes to rely on Wood for financial and emotional support as he battles his drug addiction. In return, Wood pins his hopes on Lugosi, believing that the washed-up actor will lend credibility to his films and lead him to immeasurable success.

Lugosi and Wood meet by chance in a funeral parlor, where Lugosi is trying out coffins, linking him to his most famous role as Dracula in Tod Browning's 1931 film. This scene shows Lugosi as a persona rather than an actual man with flaws and weaknesses, and it anticipates the way Wood refuses to acknowledge Lugosi's failings. Although Wood and Lugosi work together intimately throughout the film and become close companions, Wood's delusions about him persist. After Lugosi passes away, Wood is seen sitting alone in a screening room, sharing the frame with a single path of projected light. He watches the last filmed footage of Bela, a melancholy scene showing the old man slowly plucking a rose in front of an empty white house. Any of Wood's real access to Lugosi is and always has been only through celluloid.

Wood himself is perhaps the best representation of the misunderstood outcast. Anointed the "Worst Director of All Time" by Harry and Michael Medved in their 1980 book, *The Golden Turkey Awards*, the real Edward D. Wood, Jr., was an inept filmmaker who relied more on gumption than talent. His schlocky films often lacked coherent scripts, continuity, proper pacing, production values, and actors unafraid of the camera. And yet, armed with pure optimism in the face of humiliation and rejection, Burton's Ed Wood is not as naïve or out of touch as he may appear. He is the embodiment of hope, Burton's nod to the merits of not compromising. Indeed, it is easy to draw a parallel between Burton's own fortitude and Wood's brave attempts to pursue his own distinctive vision.

Burton crafts a simultaneously alienating and sympathetic portrait of the beleaguered director. In one shot, Wood's girlfriend, standing in the background, puzzles over her missing angora sweaters, while Wood's guilty visage is seen in close-up in the foreground, a vivid visualization of the cross-dresser's distance even from those closest to him. Wood is rarely on the same page as others, including his own production crew, a merry band of misfits who willingly facilitate his escapades—filming without permits on public streets, "borrowing" props from studio warehouses, or getting baptized to secure funding for a movie. After shooting only one take, Wood's cinematographer asks, "Don't you want another take for protection?" Wood replies with unabashed pride, "What's there to protect? It was perfect."

Wood genuinely aspires to be a director of Orson Welles's caliber. Instead of ridiculing him for this far-fetched ambition, Burton injects an aura of optimism in a film that documents Wood's relentless string of unquestionable failures. In a scene that provides a note of uplift, the downtrodden Wood encounters Welles in a bar, and the legendary director advises the novice never to conform to the Hollywood establishment or give up on reaching his goal, no matter how daunting the obstacles. "Ed, visions are worth fighting for. Why spend your life making someone else's dreams?"

Heeding this advice himself, Burton has been able to remain an auteur within the Hollywood system. The inherent nature of major studio productions involves the collaborative efforts of hundreds of cast and crewmembers, thereby inviting the risk of diluting one person's singular vision. However, Burton has been able to maintain his uncompromised aesthetic by working often with the same creative team, including film composer Danny Elfman, costume designer Colleen Atwood, and editor Chris Lebenzon.[13] Burton's rapport with the same actors and crew is integral to the unique texture of his films, allowing him to cultivate and develop the consistent look, sound, and style of his films with the confidence and ease that comes from trust and connection with his collaborators. Burton is the conductor at the center of this collective creativity, and his films thus far are evidence of his distinctive individual stamp. Depp summarizes succinctly, "I feel a strong connection with Tim and trust him completely. It's amazing to be invited into his world."[14]

Notes

1 The notion of the auteur, when first posited by François Truffaut in January 1954 in *Cahiers du cinéma*, treated the film director as an author, one who implements his or her vision with complete creative autonomy. Since then, the definition of the auteur has evolved to encompass filmmakers whose singular approach is distinguished by themes and styles used consistently throughout their work.

2 Most of these were films Burton directed. He developed the story and characters for *Tim Burton's The Nightmare Before Christmas*, which is directed by Henry Selick, and produced by Burton. He also developed the characters for *Tim Burton's Corpse Bride*, which he co-directed with Mike Johnson, and produced.

3 Josh Tyrangiel, "Big Fish in His Own Pond," *Time*, December 1, 2003, 90.

4 David Breskin, *Inner Views: Filmmakers in Conversation* (New York: Da Capo Press, 1997), 359.

5 Lynn Hirschberg, "Drawn to Narrative," *The New York Times Magazine*, November 9, 2003, 52.

6 *Beetlejuice* production notes.

7 David Edelstein, "Mixing Beetlejuice," *Rolling Stone*, June 2, 1988, 53.

8 Les Daniels, *Batman: The Complete History* (San Francisco: Chronicle Books, 1999), 164.

9 *Sleepy Hollow* production notes.

10 Owen Gleiberman, "Ghostmaster, Tim Burton's Big Adventure," *Boston Phoenix*, April 1, 1988, Section Three.

11 Eight of Burton's fourteen features have grossed more than $100 million worldwide.

12 Edelstein, 51.

13 Danny Elfman composed the music for *Pee-wee's Big Adventure*, "The Jar," *Alfred Hitchcock Presents* (1986), "Family Dog," *Amazing Stories* (1987), *Beetlejuice, Batman, Edward Scissorhands, Batman Returns, Tim Burton's The Nightmare Before Christmas, Mars Attacks!, Sleepy Hollow, Planet of the Apes, Big Fish, Charlie and the Chocolate Factory,* and *Tim Burton's Corpse Bride*. Colleen Atwood designed the costumes for *Edward Scissorhands, Cabin Boy* (1994), *Ed Wood, Mars Attacks!, Sleepy Hollow, Planet of the Apes, Big Fish, Sweeney Todd,* and *Alice in Wonderland*. Chris Lebenzon edited *Batman Returns, Ed Wood, Mars Attacks!, Sleepy Hollow, Planet of the Apes, Big Fish, Charlie and the Chocolate Factory, Tim Burton's Corpse Bride, Sweeney Todd,* and *Alice in Wonderland*.

14 Frank DeCaro, "A Twitchy Take on a Tale of Terror," *The New York Times*, November 14, 1999, Arts and Leisure.

1. Untitled (Man with Babies)
c. 1976–79. Ink and colored pencil on paper, 17 × 14″ (43.2 × 35.6 cm). Private collection

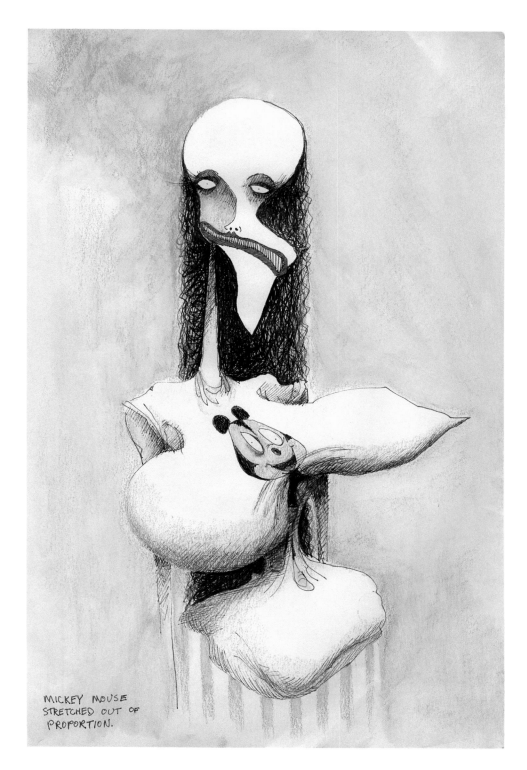

MICKEY MOUSE
STRETCHED OUT OF
PROPORTION.

2. Untitled (Girl Series)
c. 1980–84. Ink, watercolor, and crayon on paper, 14 × 9" (35.6 × 22.9 cm). Private collection

3. Untitled (Cartoons Series)
c. 1980–86. Pencil on paper, 13 × 16″ (33 × 40.6 cm). Private collection

5. Untitled (Miscellaneous)
c. 1980–84. Ink, marker, and colored pencil on paper,
10 × 9″ (25.4 × 22.9 cm). Private collection

4. Untitled (Miscellaneous)
c. 1980–84. Ink on paper, 16 × 13″ (40.6 × 33 cm). Private collection

6. Untitled (Reagan)

c. 1980–90. Ink and watercolor on paper, 8 × 4" (20.3 × 10.2 cm). Private collection

7. Untitled (Clown Series)
1993. Oil on canvas, 12 × 9″ (30.5 × 22.9 cm). Private collection

8. Untitled (*The Black Cauldron*)
1983. Ink and marker on paper, 11 × 15" (27.9 × 38.1 cm). Private collection

9. Untitled (*Creature Series*)
1998. Ink on paper, 12 × 9" (30.5 × 22.9 cm). Private collection

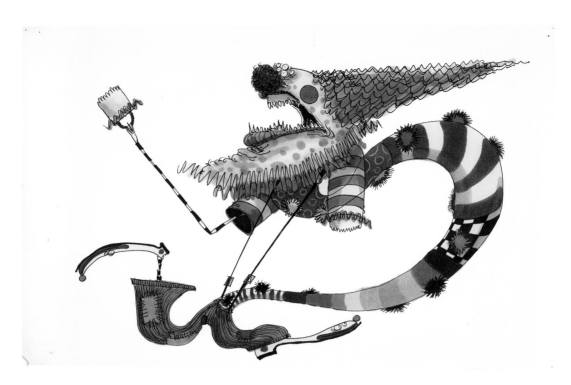

10. Untitled (Clown Series)
c. 1985–94. Ink, watercolor, and marker on paper, 11 × 16" (27.9 × 40.6 cm). Private collection

11. *Mothera*
c. 1980–88. Ink, marker, and pencil on paper, 12 ½ × 30 ½" (31.8 × 77.5 cm). Private collection

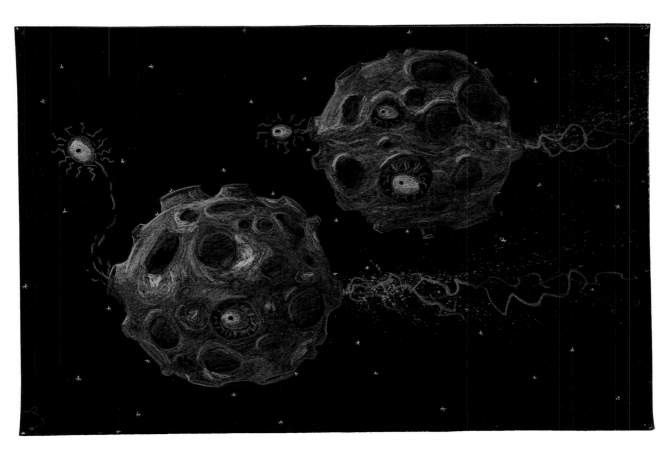

12. Untitled (*Alien*)
1983. Pastel on black paper, 12 × 18" (30.5 × 45.7 cm). Private collection

13. Untitled (Creature Series)
c. 1997–98. Pastel and acrylic on paper, 14 × 11″ (35.6 × 27.9 cm). Private collection

14. *Candy Monster* (*Trick or Treat*)
1981. Modelmaker: Rick Heinrichs. Wax, candy wrapper, wire, and paint, 9 ½ × 9 ½ × 8″ (24.1 × 24.1 × 20.3 cm). Courtesy Rick Heinrichs

15. Untitled (#6)
1982. Ink and watercolor on paper, 11 × 15" (27.9 × 38.1 cm). Private collection

16. Untitled (*Hansel and Gretel*)
1982. Ink and watercolor on paper, 11 × 12" (27.9 × 30.5 cm). Private collection

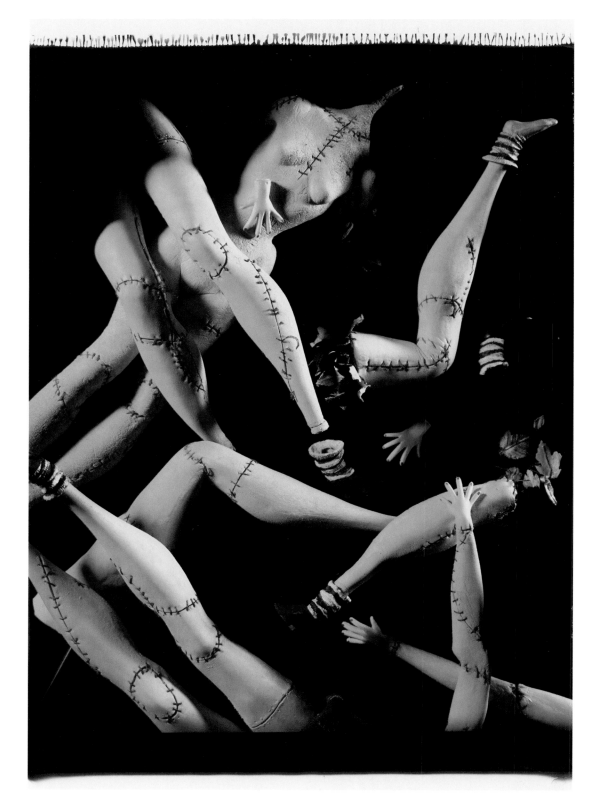

17. Untitled (Sally Parts)
1993. Polaroid, 33 × 22" (83.8 × 55.9 cm). Private collection

TEENAGER

AN AWKWARD PERIOD OF LIFE

18. Untitled (Boy Series)
c. 1980–90. Ink, marker, and watercolor on paper, 10 × 14" (25.4 × 35.6 cm). Private collection

19. Untitled (Ramone)
c. 1980–90. Ink, marker, and colored pencil on paper, 11 × 9" (27.9 × 22.9 cm). Private collection

20. Untitled (*Batman*)
1989. Pastel on paper, 12 × 9″ (30.5 × 22.9 cm). Private collection

21. Untitled (*Batman*)
1989. Ink on paper, 6 × 4″ (15.2 × 10.2 cm). Private collection

22. Untitled (*Vincent*)
1982. Ink and marker on paper, 10 × 14" (25.4 × 35.6 cm). Private collection

23. Untitled (*Trick or Treat*)
1980. Ink, marker, and colored pencil on paper, 12 × 16" (30.5 × 40.6 cm). Private collection

24. Untitled (*Vincent*)
1982. Ink on paper, 9 × 10" (22.9 × 25.4 cm). Private collection

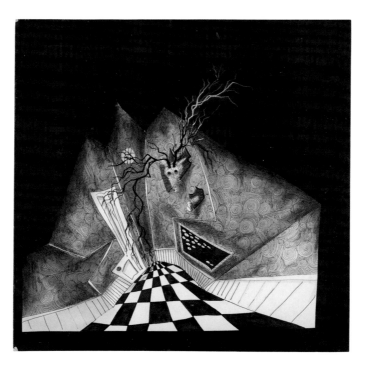

25. Untitled (*Trick or Treat*)

1980. Ink, marker, collage elements, and colored pencil on paperboard, 15 × 15" (38.1 × 38.1 cm). Private collection

26. Untitled (*Trick or Treat*)

1980. Ink and marker on paper, 15 × 12" (38.1 × 30.5 cm). Private collection

27. Untitled (*True Love*)
c. 1981–83. Ink, marker, watercolor, and colored pencil on paper, 12 × 14" (30.5 × 35.6 cm). Private collection

28. Untitled (*True Love*)
c. 1981–83. Ink, marker, and colored pencil on paper, 12 × 14" (30.5 × 35.6 cm). Private collection

29. Untitled (*Trick or Treat*)
1980. Ink and marker on paper, 10 × 13" (25.4 × 33 cm). Private collection

30. Untitled (*Romeo and Juliet*)
c. 1981–84. Ink, marker, and colored pencil on paper, 12 × 16" (30.5 × 40.6 cm). Private collection

31. Untitled (*The Melancholy Death of Oyster Boy and Other Stories*)
c. 1982–84. Ink, marker, and colored pencil on paper, 10 × 9″ (25.4 × 22.9 cm). Private collection

32. Untitled (*Edward Scissorhands*)
1990. Ink on paper, 8 × 6" (20.3 × 15.2 cm). Private collection

34. Untitled (*Tim Burton's The Nightmare Before Christmas*)
1993. Ink and crayon on paper, 8 × 5" (20.3 × 12.7 cm). Private collection

33. Untitled (*Edward Scissorhands*)
1990. Ink, watercolor, crayon, colored pencil, and correction fluid on
paper, 7 × 5" (17.8 × 12.7 cm). Private collection

35. Untitled (*Sweeney Todd*)
2006. Ink and marker on paper, 6 ¼ × 4 ½" (15.9 × 11.4 cm).
Private collection

37. Untitled (*Alice in Wonderland*)
2009. Ink and colored pencil on paper, 5 × 8" (12.7 × 20.3 cm). Private collection

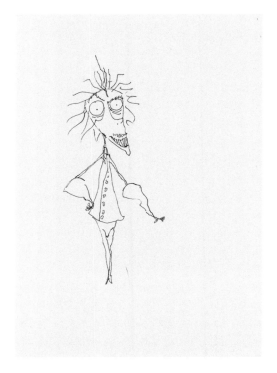

36. Untitled (*Vincent*)
1982. Ink on paper, 8 × 6" (20.3 × 15.2 cm). Private collection

38. Untitled (Corpse Boy)
1992. Acrylic on black velvet, 15 × 12" (38.1 × 30.5 cm). Private collection

39. *Clown Totem Monster* (*Trick or Treat*)
1981. Modelmaker: Rick Heinrichs. Clay, wire, and paint, 14 × 9 ½ × 8" (35.6 × 24.1 × 20.3cm). Courtesy Rick Heinrichs

40. *The Green Man*
c. 1996–98. Oil and acrylic on canvas, 10 × 8″ (25.4 × 20.3 cm). Private collection

1:75

P-2665

41. Storyboard for *Tim Burton's The Nightmare Before Christmas*
1993. Ink, marker, and colored pencil on paper, 5 × 7″ (12.7 × 17.8 cm). Private collection

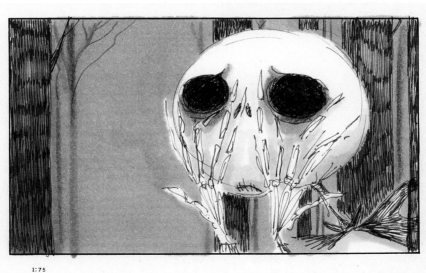

1:75

P-2665

42. Storyboard for *Tim Burton's The Nightmare Before Christmas*
1993. Ink, marker, and colored pencil on paper, 5 × 7″ (12.7 × 17.8 cm). Private collection

43. Untitled (*Trick or Treat*)
1980. Ink, marker, and colored pencil on paper. 10 × 7″ (25.4 × 17.8 cm).
Private collection

44. Untitled (*Mars Attacks!*)
1995. Watercolor on paper, 17 × 14″ (43.2 × 35.6 cm). Private collection

45. Untitled (Sunflower)
1994. Polaroid, 33 × 22" (83.8 × 55.9 cm). Private collection

the beast on the 20th floor

one night in New York,
it was really quite late.
a strange creature
climbed up the empire state.

but instead of going all
the way to the top,
it climbed 20 storys
then decided to stop.

everyone wondered
but no one could say,
why it stopped where it did
and didn't go all the way.

some thought it was scared
some thought it was tired.
some thought that maybe
it saw some one it admired.

46–49. *The Beast on the 20th Floor*
(unpublished text and concept art for *The Melancholy
Death of Oyster Boy and Other Stories*)
1997. Ink on paper, each 12 × 9″ (30.5 × 22.9 cm). Private collection

but forget what they tell you.
forget what you read.
if it goes any higher,
it's nose starts to bleed.

50. Untitled (*The World of Stainboy*)
2000. Ink, watercolor, and colored pencil on paper, 9 × 12" (22.9 × 30.5 cm). Private collection

51. *Oyster Boy*
2002. Mfr.: Gentle Giant Studios, Burbank, Ca. Two-part resin casting from clay original,
11 × 9 × 6" (27.9 × 22.9 × 15.2 cm). Courtesy Gentle Giant Studios

52. *Girl with Many Eyes*
2002. Mfr.: Gentle Giant Studios, Burbank, Ca. Two-part resin casting from clay
original, 10 × 6 × 5 ½" (25.4 × 15.2 × 14 cm). Courtesy Gentle Giant Studios

53. *Boy with Nails in Eyes*
2002. Mfr.: Gentle Giant Studios, Burbank, Ca. Two-part resin casting from clay
original, 9 × 5 × 6" (22.9 × 12.7 × 15.2 cm). Courtesy Gentle Giant Studios

54. *Blue Girl with Wine*
c. 1997. Oil on canvas, 28 × 22" (71.1 × 55.9 cm). Private collection

55. Untitled (Blue Girl with Skull)
c. 1992–99. Polaroid, 33 × 22" (83.8 × 55.9 cm). Private collection

1971

The Island of Dr. Agor.
Stop-motion short.

Houdini. Live-action short.

1972

Untitled (Tim's Dreams).
Live-action and stop-motion short.

1973

Crush Litter. Graphic design for advertising campaign. Winner of a competition sponsored by Beautiful Burbank, Inc., Burbank, Ca.

1976

The Giant Zlig. Unpublished manuscript for children's book.

1978–1979

Untitled (King and Octopus Animation).
Animated short.

1979

Stalk of the Celery Monster.
Animated short.

1980

Doctor of Doom. Live-action short.

Trick or Treat. Unrealized project.

Pirates. Unrealized project.

Toys. Unrealized project.

Luau. Live-action short.

1980–1986

Cartoon drawings.

1980–1999

Sketches, drawings, and paintings of plants, animals, people, clowns, and creatures.

1981

Little Dead Riding Hood. Unrealized project.

Cats. Unrealized project.

The Fox and the Hound. Animated feature film. Walt Disney Pictures. Directed by Ted Berman, Richard Rich, Art Stevens. Burton worked on the film as an apprentice animator.

1981–1983

True Love. Unrealized project.

1981–1984

Romeo and Juliet. Unrealized project.

1982

Numbers. Unpublished manuscript for children's book.

Tron. Feature film. Walt Disney Pictures. Directed by Steven Lisberger. Burton worked on the film as an apprentice animator.

Vincent. Animated short.
Walt Disney Pictures.

1983

Alien. Unrealized project.

Dream Factory. Unrealized project.

Hansel and Gretel. Live-action short. Disney Channel Studio Showcase/ Burton & Heinrichs Productions.

1984

Aladdin and His Wonderful Lamp.
Episode in *Shelley Duvall's Faerie Tale Theatre* series. Showtime Networks/ Gaylord Television Entertainment/ Platypus Productions/Lionsgate.

Frankenweenie. Live-action short. Walt Disney Pictures.

1985

The Black Cauldron. Animated feature film. Walt Disney Pictures. Directed by Ted Berman, Richard Rich. Burton worked on the film as a concept artist.

Pee-wee's Big Adventure. Feature film. Warner Bros. Pictures.

1986

"The Jar." Episode in *Alfred Hitchcock Presents* series. NBC Television.

1987

"**Family Dog**." Episode in *Amazing Stories* series. Amblin Television/Universal City Studios. Burton was animation designer.

1988

Beetlejuice. Feature film. Warner Bros. Pictures.

Beetlejuice: The Animated Series. Television series. ABC/Fox Television. Burton was executive producer.

1989

Batman. Feature film.
Warner Bros. Pictures.

1990

Edward Scissorhands. Feature film. Twentieth Century Fox.

Tim Burton HBO Special. Mock biography of the filmmaker promoting *Edward Scissorhands*. Created by Burton.

1992

Batman Returns. Feature film. Warner Bros. Pictures.

1992–1999

Polaroid photograph series, including Blue Girl, Christmas, *The Nightmare Before Christmas* puppets, still lifes, and Unnatural History.

1993

Tim Burton's The Nightmare Before Christmas. Animated feature film. Touchstone Pictures. Directed by Henry Selick. Burton developed the story and characters and produced the film.

Family Dog. Television series. CBS Television. Burton was executive producer and character designer.

1994

Ed Wood. Feature film. Touchstone Pictures.

Cabin Boy. Feature film. Touchstone Pictures. Directed by Adam Resnick. Burton was producer.

1995

Batman Forever. Feature film. Warner Bros. Pictures. Directed by Joel Schumacher. Burton was producer.

1996

Mars Attacks! Feature film. Warner Bros. Pictures.

James and the Giant Peach. Animated feature film. Walt Disney Pictures. Directed by Henry Selick. Burton was producer.

1997

The Melancholy Death of Oyster Boy and Other Stories. Publication. HarperCollins.

1998

Lost in Oz. Unrealized television project.

Superman Lives! Unrealized film project.

Gnome. Television commercial for Hollywood Gum.

1999

Sleepy Hollow. Feature film. Paramount Pictures.

2000

The World of Stainboy. Internet-based animated series.

Kung Fu. Television commercial for Timex.

Mannequin. Television commercial for Timex.

2001

Planet of the Apes. Feature film. Twentieth Century Fox.

2003

Big Fish. Feature film. Columbia Pictures.

2003–2009

Tragic Toys for Girls and Boys. Darkhorse Comics. Line of toys designed by Burton.

2005

Tim Burton's Corpse Bride. Animated feature film. Warner Bros. Pictures. Co-directed by Mike Johnson. Burton developed the characters and produced and directed the film.

Charlie and the Chocolate Factory. Feature film. Warner Bros. Pictures.

2006

"Bones." Music video directed by Burton, featuring The Killers. Island Records/ Def Jam Music Group.

2007

Sweeney Todd: The Demon Barber of Fleet Street. Feature film. DreamWorks Pictures/Warner Bros. Pictures.

2009

9. Feature film. Focus Features. Directed by Shane Acker. Burton was producer.

The Art of Tim Burton. Publication. Tim Burton, Inc.

2010

Alice in Wonderland. Feature film. Walt Disney Pictures.

Anderson, Kirsten, ed. *Pop Surrealism: The Rise of Underground Art*. Glendale, CA: Ignition Publishing; San Francisco: Last Gasp, 2004.

Breskin, David. *Inner Views: Filmmakers in Conversation*, New York: Da Capo Press, 1997.

Cahiers du cinéma, ed. *The Hollywood Interviews*. Oxford: Berg Publishers, 2006.

Casillas, Mercurio Lopez. *Images of Death in Mexican Prints*. Mexico: Editorial RM, 2008.

Gastman, Roger. *Juxtapoz Illustration*. Berkeley: Gingko Press, 2008.

Gavin, Francesca. *Hell Bound: New Gothic Art*. London: Laurence King Publishing Ltd., 2008.

Hirschberg, Lynn. "Drawn to Narrative," *The New York Times Magazine*, November 9, 2003.

Hyman, Timothy and Roger Malbert. *Carnivalesque*. London: Hayward Gallery Publishing, 2000.

Jordan, Matt Dukes. *Weirdo Deluxe: The Wild World of Pop Surrealism and Lowbrow Art*. San Francisco: Chronicle Books, 2005.

Klanten, Robert, Sven Ehmann, and Hendrik Hellige. *The Upset: Young Contemporary Art*. Edited by Pedro Alonzo. Berlin: Gestalten, 2008.

Linton, Meg. *In the Land of Retinal Delights: The Juxtapoz Factor*. Edited by Bolton Colburn and Robert Williams. Laguna, CA: Laguna Art Museum in association with Gingko Press, 2008.

Owens, Annie, ed. *Hi-Fructose Collected Edition*. San Francisco: Last Gasp, 2009.

Salisbury, Mark, ed. *Burton on Burton*, rev. ed. London: Faber and Faber, 2006.

Woods, Paul A., ed. *Tim Burton: A Child's Garden of Nightmares*. London: Plexus, 2007.

ACKNOWLEDGMENTS   62

We are indebted to Tim Burton for the extraordinary access he provided us to his archive, for his passionate and enlightened commitment to the exhibition and publication (as he simultaneously endured the rigors of feature film production on *Alice in Wonderland*), and for his trust in our vision. Working with his extraordinary staff—the incomparable Derek Frey, whose dedication to every aspect of *Tim Burton* was indispensable; the resourceful and creative Leah Gallo, Holly Kempf, and Albert Cuellar; and the meticulous Kory Edwards, Gene Doh, and Mo Shannon—was an experience we savored.

An exhibition as ambitious as *Tim Burton* relies on the good will and cooperation of many supporters. We are immensely grateful to Leith Adams, Ned Price, Michael Arnold, Elaine Patton, Ray Olivera, Lisa Janney, Richard Larocca, and Jeff Stevens, at Warner Bros.; Kristen McCormick, Lella Smith, Mary Walsh, Daryl Maxwell, Fox Carney, Doug Engalla, Jackie Vasquez, and Elvie Delfin, at the Disney Animation Research Library; Karl Meyer, Brian Sunderlin, Mark Waelti, Stephen Casa, Charity Talmadge, and Marilin Martin, at Gentle Giant Studios; Colleen Atwood; Rick and Dawn Heinrichs; Carlos Grangel, Jordi Grangel, and Carles Burges, at Grangel Studio; Gianna Babando and Schawn Belston, at Twentieth Century Fox; Ian Mackinnon, Peter Saunders, Gareth Richards, and Sara Mullock, at Mackinnon and Saunders; Stephen Chiodo, Edward Chiodo, and Charles Chiodo, at Chiodo Bros. Productions, Inc.; Karen Winston; Joe Maddalena at Profiles in History; Lindsay McGowan, Laurie Charchut, and Lyndel Pedersen, at Legacy Effects; Rebecca Cline and Rob Klein, at the Disney Corporate Archives; and Ron Magid. Our thanks to them all are boundless.

Much appreciated organizational aid came from Marie-Josée Kravis, MoMA President; John Lasseter, Elyse Klaidman, Christine Freeman, and Jerome Ranft, at Pixar Animation Studios; Cort Tramontin, at CK Studios; Anita Nelson, at Dark Horse Comics; Melissa Karaban, at Danny Elfman's office; Nina Rodriguez, at Expresión En Corto, IFF; and Geoff Brown, Clint Edwards,

Steven Higgins, Martin Humphries, Charles Solomon, and Catherine Surowiec. Special thanks are due to our exhibition tour partners: at the Australian Centre for the Moving Image, Melbourne, Tony Sweeney and Conrad Bodman; and at the Bell Lightbox, Toronto, Noah Cowan.

At The Museum of Modern Art, for their enduring faith and encouragement, we thank Director Glenn D. Lowry, Associate Director Kathy Halbreich, Senior Deputy Director of Exhibitions Jennifer Russell, Senior Deputy Director of Curatorial Affairs Peter Reed, Chief Operating Officer James Gara, and Senior Deputy Director of External Affairs Michael Margitich.

Tim Burton would not have been possible without the involvement of Jennifer Wolfe, Ramona Bannayan, Susan Palamara, Allison Needle, Jeri Moxley, Kristen Shirts, Rob Jung, Sarah Wood, Rachel Abrams, Jack Siman, Erik Landsberg, Robert Kastler, and Roberto Rivera (Collection Management and Exhibition Registration); Paul Jackson, Kim Mitchell, Margaret Doyle, and Daniela Stigh (Communications); Jim Coddington, Roger Griffith, and Ana Martins (Conservation); Todd Bishop, Mary Hannah, Lauren Stakias, Rebecca Stokes, Jason Persse, Amy Gordon, Tamsin Nutter, and Zoe Jackson (Development and Membership); Wendy Woon, Pablo Helguera, Laura Beiles, Elizabeth Margulies, Sara Bodinson, Nathan Sensel, Beth Harris, Cari Frisch, and Marit Dewhurst (Education); Jennifer Manno Cohen, Maria DeMarco Beardsley, Jessica Cash, and Emily Scaros (Exhibition Administration); Jerry Neuner, David Hollely, Michele Arms, Peter Perez, Polly Lai, Cynthia Kramer, Carlos Carcamo, William Ashley, John Martin, and Matt Osiol (Exhibition Design and Production); Jan Postma (Finance); Nancy Adelson and Patty Lipshutz (General Counsel); Ingrid Chou, Claire Corey, and Inva Cota (Graphic Design); Charles Kalinowski, K Mita, Howard Deitch, Mike Gibbons, Lucas Gonzalez, Nathaniel Longcope, Hayna Garcia, Tal Marks, Steven Warrington, Edmund D'Inzillo, Greg Singer, Zdenek Kriz, Allegra Burnette, David Hart, and Chiara Bernasconi (Information Technology);

Julia Hoffmann, Julie Welch, and Victor Samra (Marketing); Diana Pulling and Eliza Ryan (Office of the Director); Richard Mawhinney and Nelson Nieves (Operations); Christopher Hudson, Kara Kirk, David Frankel, Christina Grillo, Marc Sapir, Rebecca Roberts, Hannah Kim, Carey Gibbons, Amanda Washburn, catalogue editor Claire Barliant, and designer Roy Brooks (Publications); Kathy Thornton-Bias, Lauren Solotoff, Dawn Bossman, Norman Laurila, Bonnie Mackay, Seok-Hee Lee, and Ray Martinelli (Retail); Ron Simoncini (Security); Nicholas Apps, Elizabeth Pizzo, Paola Zanzo, Bic Leu, and Olivia Striffler (Special Programming and Events); and Diana Simpson, Lynn Parish, Melanie Monios, Marjorie Perez, Sonya Shrier, and Jean Mary Bongiorno (Visitor Services).

We are fortunate to have the support of our inestimable colleagues in the Department of Film: Sally Berger, Kitty Cleary, Dave Friedman, Andy Haas, Jytte Jensen, Laurence Kardish, Mary Keene, Nancy Lukacinsky, Anne Morra, Justin Rigby, Laura Rugarber, Josh Siegel, Charles Silver, Katie Trainor, Pierre Vaz, Arthur Wehrhahn, John Weidner, and Peter Williamson; and in particular, our department manager Sean Egan, and our dedicated interns Gabrielle Stowe, Wayne Titus, Alice Remsnyder, and Elizabeth Quilter.

And finally we express our gratitude to Syfy, whose generous financial support allowed us to make this celebration of imagination and creativity a reality.

Ron Magliozzi, Assistant Curator, Jenny He, Curatorial Assistant, and Rajendra Roy, The Celeste Bartos Chief Curator, Department of Film

Published in conjunction with the exhibition *Tim Burton*, organized by Ron Magliozzi, Assistant Curator, and Jenny He, Curatorial Assistant, Department of Film, with Rajendra Roy, The Celeste Bartos Chief Curator of Film.

Imagine Greater

Tim Burton is sponsored by Syfy.

Produced by the Department of Publications, The Museum of Modern Art, New York

Edited by Claire Barliant
Designed by Roy Brooks, Fold Four
Production by Christina Grillo
Printed and bound by Dr. Cantz'sche Druckerei, Ostfildern, Germany

This book is typeset in Foundry Form Sans and Lo Type. The paper is 150 gsm Luxosamt offset.

Published by The Museum of Modern Art, 11 W. 53 Street, New York, New York 10019

© 2009 The Museum of Modern Art, New York
Third printing, 2009

Distributed in the United States and Canada by D.A.P./Distributed Art Publishers, Inc., New York
Distributed outside the United States and Canada by Thames & Hudson Ltd, London

Library of Congress Control Number: 2009933514
ISBN: 978-0-87070-760-5

Cover: Untitled (*The Melancholy Death of Oyster Boy and Other Stories*). c. 1982–84. Ink, marker, and colored pencil on paper, 10 × 9" (25.4 × 22.9 cm). Private collection. See plate 31

Back cover: *Blue Girl with Wine*. c. 1997. Oil on canvas, 28 × 22" (71.1 × 55.9 cm). Private collection. See plate 54

Printed in Germany